# LETTERS TO THE VALLEY

# DAVID MAS MASUMOTO

# LETTERS TO THE VALLEY

# A HARVEST OF MEMORIES

Illustrated by Doug Hansen

Great Valley Books ⋅ Heyday Books, Berkeley, California

First paperback printing 2007

Paperback ISBN: 1-59714-038-4

*Library of Congress Cataloging-in-Publication Data*
Masumoto, David Mas.
  Letters to the valley : a harvest of memories / David Mas Masumoto ; illustrated by Doug Hansen.
    p. cm. — (A Great Valley Book)
  ISBN 1-890771-86-4 (hardcover : alk. paper)
  1. Masumoto, David Mas. 2. Farmers—California—Del Ray—Biography.
3. Japanese-American Farmers—California—Del Rey—Biography. 4. Farm life—California—Del Rey. 5. Family farms—California—Del Rey. 6. Del Rey (Calif.)—Social life and customs. I. Title. II. Series.
  SB63.M36A3 2004
  630'.92--dc22
                              2004007029

Book design by Rebecca LeGates
Orders, inquiries, and correspondence should be addressed to:
    Heyday Books
    P.O. Box 9145, Berkeley, CA 94709
    (510) 549-3564, fax (510) 549-1889
    www. heydaybooks.com

Printed in China by Imago

10 9 8 7 6 5 4 3 2 1

CONTENTS

Introduction . . . . . . . . . . . . . . . . . . . . . . . . . . . . .ix

Part One: Letters from a Farmer . . . . . . . . . . 1
  Talking with Grapevines . . . . . . . . . . . . . . . 3
  Names from Our Past . . . . . . . . . . . . . . . . 9
  Spring Plowing . . . . . . . . . . . . . . . . . . . . . 15
  Ghosts in the Fields . . . . . . . . . . . . . . . . 21
  Scent of a Father . . . . . . . . . . . . . . . . . . 29
  Lizard Dance . . . . . . . . . . . . . . . . . . . . . . 35
  Hunger for Memory. . . . . . . . . . . . . . . . . 41

Part Two: Family Letters. . . . . . . . . . . . . . . 47
  Spring Weeds . . . . . . . . . . . . . . . . . . . . . . 49
  The T-Shirt Scale. . . . . . . . . . . . . . . . . . . 55
  Holiday Meals . . . . . . . . . . . . . . . . . . . . . 61
  Big Fat Envelopes . . . . . . . . . . . . . . . . . . 67
  Advice to Farm Kids . . . . . . . . . . . . . . . 73
  Becoming a Soldier. . . . . . . . . . . . . . . . . . 79

Part Three: Community Correspondence . . . 85

    Baseball Saved Us. . . . . . . . . . . . . . . . . . . . . 87

    Old Friends. . . . . . . . . . . . . . . . . . . . . . . . . 93

    Hardpan . . . . . . . . . . . . . . . . . . . . . . . . . . . 99

    Passion to Learn. . . . . . . . . . . . . . . . . . . . . 105

    The Other California. . . . . . . . . . . . . . . . . 111

    The Good Neighbor . . . . . . . . . . . . . . . . . 117

    How to Write a Letter. . . . . . . . . . . . . . . . 125

Acknowledgments . . . . . . . . . . . . . . . . . . . . . 131

*To those who still write letters and love to read them*
David Mas Masumoto


*To Ray Pool, of Madera, California—*
*the farmer in my family*
Doug Hansen

Also by David Mas Masumoto

*Four Seasons in Five Senses: Things Worth Savoring*
*Harvest Son: Planting Roots in American Soil*
*Epitaph for a Peach: Four Seasons on My Family Farm*
*Country Voices: The Oral History of a Japanese*
   *American Family Farm Community*
and the CD *Story Songs*

Also by Doug Hansen

*Fresno Sketchbook*
*Fresno Sketchbook II*

# Letter to a Friend

JANUARY

Dear Charlie,

You're my editor at the *Fresno Bee* and when we first talked about my writing for the newspaper, something you said stuck with me. You said you'd once read that creating a good column is like writing a letter to a friend.

Letter writing: The simple act of committing thoughts to words, capturing observations and feelings, sharing them with others so they may be read and reread.

I remember my *baachan's* (grandmother's) stack of cherished letters, wrapped in a yellowed linen cloth and stored in her dresser. As a kid, I stared at the funny-looking Japanese kanji calligraphy, wondering how anyone could make sense of those little squiggly lines, black dots and dashes. Years later when I first attempted to write our family name in Japanese and asked Baachan for help, I made a painful discovery: she could not write.

She gamely tried. Her old hand shook and her fingers turned white as she gripped the pencil tightly. The lead point pierced the paper and tore through, leaving behind a few rough scratches. She put the pencil down and looked away.

Later I realized that not only was she unable to write her name, she also could not read. She came to America as a farmworker and stayed a farmworker. Writing and reading were not important to a small farm girl in 1900. Yet she still clung to a handful of letters—words on paper, scratches that carried meaning and memories.

When I started writing these newspaper essays, I wondered if readers would be interested in letters from a forty-eight-year-old Japanese American working on a family farm. My wife, Marcy, knows of farm life. She grew up on a goat dairy in the high desert of Southern California, her family transplanted from the small dairies of Wisconsin. Our daughter, Nikiko, a teenager hungry to see the world beyond this Valley, and my son, Korio, not quite a teenager, who reminds me of my youth when I'd rather play than work, both know of their father's work: farmers often can't keep secrets, our work is public.

I write as a native son and an outsider, born in Selma, a small town just south of Fresno. The Masumotos labored in these fields for three generations, my grandparents immigrating from Japan at the beginning of the 1900s, settling in the Central Valley with dreams of harvests and prosperity. My father bought our farm in 1948 after returning from the Gila River, Arizona, Relocation Center of World War II, where he had met my mother.

But I couldn't wait to escape this Valley and longed for something better beyond the mountains. I ran off to the University of California at Berkeley, knowing it would be a college campus my parents would never visit (they didn't). And I had no intention of ever returning. As if the big city wasn't far enough away, I then journeyed to Japan for two years as an exchange student, spending half the time in the small rural village outside of Kumamoto that Baachan had left decades earlier and to which she never returned. I rediscovered the very thing I was trying to escape:

farming. Yet the circle was not complete until I came back to the California family farm in 1980.

A writing teacher once challenged me: who cares about all this? I hope readers want to know more about where their food comes from and those who grow the bounty. I believe people still have a memory of the real flavor of a juicy summer peach and a luscious nectarine.

This is not just a farm, it's about farming organically and facing the challenges and labors when working with nature. This is not a factory in the fields but something alive and dynamic: taste the salt of sweat and the geography of dust; witness the power of a hail storm to devastate democratically; sigh with the depression of low market prices and the rot of unharvested crops—the real flavors of a farm.

And at the heart lies family, generations staying put and planting roots. Family memories connect us in a universal way, from food traditions during holiday gatherings to advice from parents to children. Stories bind us to a place and each other. In addition to peaches and grapes, I grow family stories.

My letters, Charlie, are from a place you and many others call home. The Central Valley of California, a 400-mile-long, 50-mile-wide valley in the heart of California. Protected by the Sierra Nevada towering to the east and the low coastal ranges to the west, agriculture dominates the landscape but our cities continue to grow—close to a million people live within fifty miles of our farm.

Yet a small-town mentality still dominates the landscape. I've often thought of this Valley as a series of villages connected by an asphalt river called Highway 99. We accept our shortcomings and have learned to live with imperfection, a wonderfully simple and naive perspective, strangely comfortable as we raise our families and grow old. Good enough to call home, not bad enough to talk of escape: a place people plan to stay a while. I recall amazing my friends as I finished college and we exchanged addresses—I'd have the same one for the rest of my life.

Because it's home, many of us do care, and I hope we care more. Too many of our problems remain invisible and many keep a safe distance from things that trouble us—remnants, I suppose, from a rural lifestyle and getting along with lifelong neighbors.

But things are changing rapidly with population growth and a shifting agricultural economy. Years ago, as I began to farm organically, weeds rapidly overtook the farm. My neighbors grew concerned and one finally stopped to talk with Marcy, wondering if something had happened to me, because "the farm looked like the

farmer had died." Perhaps I did. And now I share stories with these neighbors as we struggle to redefine
our place on this land.

I write letters to describe the spiritual geography of
a place. I journey with words and the hope my stories
travel beyond our valley. Food and family, neighbors
and community. A book of letters, a hunger for stories,
a harvest of memory.

Thanks for listening.

Mas

# ONE

# Letters from a Farmer

I write literary field notes. Returning to our eighty-acre family farm, I wanted to work the land and harvest words. When doing tractor work, I used to jot thoughts in the dust on fenders. But by the end of the row they'd be covered and lost; how appropriate for a beginner writer. I soon learned to take a notepad with me. My words join a rich tradition of farmers writing letters. Reflections by a farmer, a settler; not the visitor passing through nor the journalist without roots. Stories of the land, pondering the meaning of our work and family, reflections of our life in words. By writing letters we tell the world that we trust our stories and are willing to share them with others. We find a power in these places and the things that grow here.

# Talking with Grapevines

Dear Dad,

Now I know why you're the first to go out and prune the vineyards every year. You're a farmer caught in a ritual of nature, a cycle of life, a rite of passage from one year to the next. In your eightieth season, pruning is like revisiting old friends. Our Thompsons were planted four years before you were born; I suppose it's rejuvenating to work with something always older than you. If they can be productive year after year, why not old farmers?

Like many farmers, you have always been a quiet man—but do you talk with the grapevines? In the fields do you have conversations as the dew and fog drip from the stakes, your pruning shears snip with a steady pace and the trellis wire screeches when you yank old canes, trying to unravel and free them?

The vines seem silent during their annual haircut and stand comfortably resting during their winter dormancy. As you pause to examine a vine, I believe you're talking to yourself, trying to discover the history and hear the story in each. In the coarse and gnarled black bark, with twisted and contorted ancient trunks, you'll find the pruning scars from generations. Some wounds you left a decade ago—or was it two?—when you radically decided to reshape the vine, the crown growing too far from the stake, a lopsided vine that would only continue on its crooked path.

So you cut off half, gave up part of a harvest that season, and a healthy vine now hugs the stake with strong, balanced growth. You knew the secret of sacrifice.

Good pruning is really the art of taking away, like a sculptor chiseling at a rock, working to uncover life inside. You pace around the grapevine, pause and clip, lean in and cut; eyes dart back and forth, searching for the strong canes and locating spurs for next year's growth. You work with the past and see the future— adding to a living timeline.

The dialogue between farmer and vine must be slow and engaging. It takes time to get to know a vine, to pay attention to the nuances of each one. A farmer's relationship with the land grows by gradual accrual, punctuated by the annual rites of pruning, watering and harvesting. And I've discovered a secret you've known for years: Work with the intention of returning the next year and the year after that. Imagine how the world would be better if we all grew relationships with such intention.

Farmers must talk to vines and trees because the work is isolating, our twenty- or forty-acre islands not even close enough to shout across a field to neighbors. (We do know, though, how to wave across a field. Hand slowly rises, a broad sweep of the arm, then pause for a second of recognition.) Most of the time we labor alone, independent of others, and enjoy the solitude. In winter I prune in the fog, protected from the rest of the world, safe and secure with my companions.

Gardeners must feel the same when they retreat to their backyard beds, speaking with flowers, cajoling the buds or cursing the weeds. I imagine garden and keeper sometimes sigh together and engage in silent conversations, sorting out family dynamics and working through relationships. I know of some doctors and nurses who garden, a respite from the medical world of healing and crises into another natural universe of uncontrolled wonder. I'm not sure they'd call it escape. Both worlds embody success and challenge; perhaps they are complementary, helping us all understand that at times failure is part of life.

I'm learning to talk with the vines. Usually I ask how they feel and request a warning if there's a problem with mildew, worms or a short crop. The grapes dangle quietly and, if I'm lucky, the leaves respond with a rustle. I know. I know. You can't always control things. I'm reminded that these are living things, not machines or factories in the fields.

Is this crazy—talking to grapes and peaches and nectarines? Time to grow up. This is about making money. Perhaps I've been out alone on the farm too long and need to get into town a little more often. But why can't you still enjoy yourself too? We can take this profession much too seriously. Talking with the vines—either the first sign of losing a grip on reality or of finding renewed comfort in a chosen lifestyle.

I look at old farmers out early each winter, trudging into fields with shears in hand. Snip, cut, slice. Vine after vine. They prune a little each day, keeping themselves busy I suppose, and witness daily accomplishments with a sense of productivity. They look content.

It's like visiting a cemetery and talking with neighbors who have passed on, only these fields are still alive, and farmers honor that moment. I believe old farmers fool nature. By pruning each winter, they speak clearly: they intend to see the grapes all the way through one more summer and one more harvest.

A whisper I'm beginning to understand as I too become an old farmer and learn to talk with my vines.

Your son,
Dave Mas

# Names from Our Past

Dear Dad,

I have been thinking of the names of old peach varieties that few people grow anymore:

Elberta. J. H. Hale. Red Haven.

These old fruits lacked full color and shelf life, qualities more and more fruit brokers and produce managers claimed were needed. And consumer dollars rewarded newer varieties bred for lipstick-red color and could stay rock hard for weeks in cold storage after harvest. Who cared about taste when they looked so good? Old fruits were deemed obsolete along with their farmers.

Now as I farm and cling to varieties I grew up with (Sun Crest peaches and Le Grand nectarines), which mostly are gone from the Valley's fields, mine seem like memorials to the past. I too am feeling old and forgotten.

Once while cleaning up after a long day's work, I found, tucked up high on a shelf in our barn, an old tin coffee can where you saved the hand stamps from our fruit-packing days.

Rio Oso Gem. Sun Grand. Late Le Grand.

I read aloud those names as the evening gave way to darkness. It felt like citing a list of our neighbor farmers who had passed on: Kamm Oliver, Kei Hiyama, Al Riffel.

But these hand stamps are different, and they are part of my history too. Every summer I lived with them, pressing the names onto wooden boxes. The stamps' wooden handles were worn smooth from use over the years. The rubber lettering gradually collected saw dust and had to be periodically cleaned out with a nail. My fingers wore perpetual purple ink stains, and one summer I spent weeks with "Forty-niner"—a cling peach—embossed on my arm like a farmboy's tattoo.

Names from our past. A simpler time when we knew all the peaches' names because there were only a few. Stores used to advertise by variety, and families held annual gatherings centered on fruits. I've heard that Elbertas brought generations of women together to can and jam: an American quilt of food that we contributed to each year.

Ironically, with dozens of varieties and new ones introduced annually, fruits today are rarely sold by name. Peaches are now simply peaches and we have lost our identity in a generic marketplace.

Of course, some varieties had flaws and prone-to-split pits or small size. Others overly sensitive to weather swings—a cool spring might produce a funny shape or a heat wave prior to harvest could promote a soft and easily bruised tip. All reasons why some old varieties have fallen aside, doomed in a modern marketplace that seems to reward size, looks and shelf life. We live in a world that wants young peaches and nectarines.

But these stamps connect me with a time and place, and echo with reminders of our family farm. You've taught me well, Dad. I still farm with a passion for taste, hoping my fruits create that moment of recognition in the middle of long summer days, a pause to enjoy something with flavor.

We farm memories—fruits that catapult someone into remembrances of things past: a story of eating a fresh Babcock peach or greengage plum. If our work is done correctly, it's no longer about our fruits but rather a personalized story of flavor.

I want to believe people still have a memory of great peaches. It's probably an older generation who knows what sweet, juicy ones taste like. And I hope they don't forget.

I worry about children growing up without an appreciation of these flavors. They don't know the taste of a great peach or nectarine or plum. All their knowledge is based on what they've been exposed to: a peach-flavored jelly bean or fruit roll-up. Sugar sweetness all too often becomes their criteria in judging taste.

As a result, old varieties become homeless. Without memory, there is no sense of what is lost. Sun Crest and Le Grand become secrets, and the world doesn't need any more secrets.

Dad, I just might find a way to use these old stamps and perhaps add some new ones to our farm family.

Nubiana. Flavortop. Nectar.

They sound wonderful, like poetry, and make me feel young. Perhaps that's why you kept the stamps all these years in that old coffee can.

And so will I.

Your son,
Dave Mas

*Author note: What was your favorite variety of peach, nectarine or plum? I'm always searching and want to plant some memories on my farm. Let me know at masumotobee@aol.com.*

# Spring Plowing

Dear Mr. Muira,

Spring awakens in our valley with the sun's warmth on our cheeks and a stirring of life within. We forget that other places still have snow, with threats of late spring frosts that hunt like a stalking wolf, howling reminders to both farmers and gardeners that winter isn't quite through.

But in our valley we are fortunate: life starts early.

You're an old farmer who can't retire from growing things and now have moved your itch to a city home and backyard. Farmers and gardeners share a spring calling: a longing to get outside, breathe in the air and touch the earth with our hands. We want to feel the damp soil under our fingernails, long to break winter's crust and turn the soil as if we free a spirit in the land.

With the first signs of spring, we plow the earth and it plows something into us.

Growing things seems natural, a distinctly human act, part of our desire to reflect, build and create. But nurturing seems out of place in our fast-paced, high-tech information age. Gardens foster connections based on slow timelines, much like learning.

I've often thought all students and teachers should be required to grow something, to understand the patience required and the long learning curves of development. We all could benefit from planting seeds with patience to see the flowers bloom.

I sometimes fantasize: What if all professions required that you know how to garden? Could we be better off if businesspeople, lawyers, doctors and politicians had to first pass a gardening test? Humility might be fostered alongside some humbling harvests.

Your gardens, Mr. Muira, help connect you to a real presence. I can tell as you prune a bonsai pine, skillfully guiding the clipper by feeling the needles with your hands and fingers and quickly snipping off unwanted growth. You could prune blindfolded, allowing a touch world to guide you. That's the secret calling of spring: we allow the senses back into our lives.

After the cold of winter and our thick blankets protecting us, we take off gloves and shed our clothes, wanting to feel weather with our skin: a tactile relationship. We seek to touch something and be touched in return—like a good hug.

The world of touch has become alien in our modern society. I find the seasons sometimes blurring together as I seek to insulate myself from the cold or heat as if to say, "Damn the weather, life should unfold someplace between 68 and 72 degrees!"

I too often ignore opportunities for touch to have meaning, as if I've been programmed not to pay attention. The great eating revolution of my generation has been fast food and the doing away of silverware. Yet I can't recall the sensation of a sesame bun or the feel of a french fry on my fingertips. We eat with our hands and have no memory of it.

Spring offers a reprieve, a chance to redeem myself and sharpen my senses. I connect with old friends:

shovels, rakes and pruning shears that sat quietly in the corner of the shed all winter, ignored and forgotten. I imagine their feelings are hurt, but rationalize my neglect by believing that old garden and farm tools must hibernate and rest, waiting out the cold, trusting that following harsh winters will come spring. Then I run my hand along wood handles, cool and sleek to touch. I add my own body oils, leaving my mark as we warm up for spring work. A season of renewal for us all.

First contact with the spring earth, we stimulate all our senses. I like to think of this as an annual ritual. My eyes initially tell me the seasons have changed with more sunlight, less fog, longer days. Then I touch the damp earth and feel spring. Close up I can smell something rich, almost fattening, like an aroma of chocolate. This must be dessert.

Pause and stop. At first I hear nothing, then my breathing. I become lost in thoughts of a garden growing, a farm flush with green: the vegetables, fruits, grapes and harvest. My mouth waters in anticipation. Spring has sprung.

Later, I spy the first green shoots and realize they are weeds. They won't let me forget the work and the sweat. But I also continue to enjoy the moment, for these are not yet weeds, just misplaced plants. All green, the color of spring marking the end of winter.

Too quickly my moment of rhapsody passes with a reality check and the growing list of chores: beds to prepare, fields to plow, things to plant. This is about real work.

So then how do I begin the spring? I rub my hands together and chant: "This is a season to get dirty."

Good growing,
Mas

# Ghosts in the Fields

Dear Dad,

I work with the ghosts of farmworkers. They haunt me, mostly in the winter, when the tule fog hugs the earth for days. I trudge to the fields, forcing myself to venture into the wet, bone-chilling cold, listening to the moisture drip from the peach trees and grapevines. That's when the ghosts greet me: a shadow in the gray mist, something familiar in the distance, moving methodically among the grapevines, a fellow worker lost in the white glare of winters.

Our family were not always farmers. You and Mom, Jiichan and Baachan (grandpa and grandma) all started in the fields. Farmworkers, generations from foreign lands, brought into California to work the land.

Working alongside an army of common laborers, you changed our valley's natural desert into a garden. Ghosts who leveled the uneven earth, planted trees and vines, dug irrigation ditches and canals, brought wealth and prosperity to a barren soil in exchange for cheap wages. Like all farmworkers, you were invisible.

But like many, you also carried a dream of progressing from laborer to owner, of becoming a farmer. Dad, when you were a laborer, did you feel exploited? Is that why you had such a hunger to own a piece of this land?

Our family managed to rent land, made and lost some money and eventually scraped enough together to get a place of our own right after World War II.

"Too much risk!" Baachan chastised. "At least as a farmworker, you would get paid," she cautioned.

The ghosts of farmers and workers looked similar then, both hunched over in the fields with hoe or shovel in the blistering heat of our summers, or huddled around a small vine-stump field fire in the middle of winter, trying to get feeling back into fingers and hands before venturing back to pruning. Some years our family pruned a neighbor's orchard or vineyard to earn cash, then came home late in the day or at the end of the season to do our own place. Later, when you became the farmer and hired help, I saw you go out and work side by side with the pruners or pickers.

You respected them because you were once one of them. A Latino friend who grew up in the fields says he respected those farmers who worked with their crews, everyone sharing the dust and taste of sweat as class lines blurred.

Farmworker ghosts have left their mark on the vines, pruning scars from generations that helped shape our farm. A good year meant more work as additional acres were planted. Prosperity did seem to trickle down to all and I'm not haunted as much by these ghosts.

Baachan died more than ten years ago. Her mind failed long before the muscles hardened from years of battling johnsongrass. Today, especially during the last light of day, I occasionally see a dark shadow trudging down a dirt avenue or slouching over on the horizon along the ditch bank. I think it's her spirit, still walking lands she worked but never owned; the lost soul of a field-worker who never grew rich while the land grew fat with harvests. Searching, but never fulfilled.

Now I'm the farmer who hires workers who help me. Dad, only a few of today's workers have your dreams of farming here in California. The economic landscape has changed vividly. The price of land, the capital investment required, and the larger and larger economics of scale create barriers to ownership. A few workers do have places of their own in Mexico, but most just come here in search of a job. They're another wave of labor from a foreign land, paid to grow our foods and stay in the shadows. Am I now the boss and exploiter?

I can defend myself, claiming to provide jobs for those hungry to earn a living. The working conditions remain gruesome, our twenty-one days in a row of record heat over 100 degrees this past summer—right in the middle of our peach harvest—a painful reminder of farming's reality. Ripe peaches don't wait for pleasant days; nature dictates working conditions. Yet workers came, sweated and took home money. Many send their earnings back to their homelands. Our little country post office annually ships millions of dollars in money orders to small, rural villages in remote areas of Mexico. Our valley in California supports another valley thousands of miles away.

I can also explain that in our country, we have a cheap-food policy. Americans spend less on food than any other nation in the world. Every year farmers try to grow more efficiently and more productively, chasing after the fewer and fewer dollars that the public is willing to spend. All the while, we face more and more competition. Farmers live at the mercy of the marketplace: we grow a product, commit our labor and pay up front with no idea of the price we may receive.

Paying more for labor cannot be simply an expense that farmers pass on to the consumer.

Drive out into our countryside and you will see another vineyard pulled out, grapes yanked from the earth, roots ripped from our valley, vines that can produce heavy harvests but with prices that no longer support the effort. Each block of vines, a small forty-acre farm with the farmer probably in his sixties or seventies, is land that now sits idle. Invisible are the lost wages of a farmworker who could have pruned, irrigated, weeded and harvested: $30,000 to $40,000 in wages ripped from our local economy for each such farm. Money earned never more.

Perhaps the ghosts of today's farmers and workers haven't changed that much from those of the past. Both are caught in a system that beats you down with physical work—a world full of risk and at the whims of nature, but without the potential for huge rewards. The spirit of farming haunts me with a cold, gripping chill of reality: to grow old alone, to die tired.

Dad, I wish there was a simple answer, but rarely do the unseen garner attention. As leaders in the Valley focus on attracting new industry and better-paying jobs, I hope they don't forget our agrarian roots and the family farms. We still have a multibillion-dollar industry that generates well-paying, skilled jobs. These farms are not plantations with lords and slaves.

Yet agriculture is still supported on the backs of low-wage earners. The ghosts who help grow our food will always be around. Wishing they'd go away would only drive them from our valley into another country, and whose loss would that be?

I dream of improving working conditions on our small farm and offering better-paying jobs. The "living wage movement"—a small, fledgling idea to pay workers more so they can move beyond poverty and into a new economy based on what people are worth, not simply trying to pay the least—has generated some interest. I've seen this make inroads in the coffee industry. "Fair Trade Coffee" is a branded product for which consumers often pay more, to know that those who grow the coffee and work the fields are getting a living wage.

"Fair trade" with progressive peaches or radical raisins? An agriculture driven by consumers who are willing to pay more because they know the story of their food and how paying pennies more per pound can reward those who work the land. "Feel-good economics"? Yep. After all, isn't that what's at the soul of food? Eat to feel good?

I have no answer and have been criticized because I can't figure it all out. Some will scoff at my fair-trade idealism. But I think those skeptics haven't worked around the invisible lately.

The ghosts of past, present and future stay with me in the fields. Perhaps my calling is to tell a tale of workers on the land and the story of the silent hands and unseen faces behind our foods. One day, I too will become a ghost.

Your son,
Mas

OCTOBER

# Scent of a Father

Dear Dad,

Someone once asked me how I would remember you. My answer: Probably by your scent.

Then they asked, What does your father smell like? My answer: Like the smoke from a campfire.

Ironically, I have never gone camping with you. We have never spent overnight bonding trips together out in the wilderness. Yet whenever I smell wood burning or stand for any length of time near a fire and allow the smoke to linger and penetrate my clothes, I think of you.

In the old orchard that we planted three decades ago, every year branches and limbs die. Throughout the season, we saw and drag them to the ditch bank, and in the winter, when there's finally some time to finish a chore, we burn the woodpile, a precursor to pruning for the next year and a time of renewal.

Most small farms have to have a woodpile, a collection of limbs and stumps mixed with odd clippings and prunings from the fields and yard. A place to stack the dead—trees and vines that have aged or, when grafting, the old branches that were sawed and hauled off in order to make way for the new. Tucked away out back, these piles tell of changes on our farm. It's a modern-day slash-and-burn method. As the farm evolves, burning is like a purification ritual as the old turns into ashes. Sometimes I'll spread the dust in the fields when the cremation pile rises high.

Dad, remember when we headed out early one day with pruning shears, shovel, and handsaw, along with some sheets of newspaper and a book of matches? You had a routine of waiting for the rare day when the wind blew from the east to west, to keep smoke out of our eyes. Then you found a dry branch, cut it into smaller kindling and crumpled newspaper around it. At the flick of a match, the pile ignited into flames, and quickly the fire leaped up and the dry, withering leaves exploded in a crackle. The slender and well-cured branches caught fire and then the entire pile jumped to life. The smoke was thick and dense—the smell choking and

the heat intense. The smoke penetrated my lungs. I could no longer smell the fire; I felt enveloped.

We spent the whole day together, talking little and instead listening to the hiss and crack of the wood and the popping and spitting sap. We stood in silence and watched with a shiver of terror at the power of the flames—a humbling feeling before the fury.

Occasionally, the smell of burnt rubber piqued my interest. The aroma was strong, distinct and nasty. I learned to look immediately at my work boots—had I stepped on another ember? Once I had to retreat from the fire and take off my shoes.

I tapped the soles and they were so hot I couldn't keep my fingers on their surface. I felt my socks—they too were flushed. Had I kept my boots on, I would have burnt my feet, my shoes on fire without flames, the scent of melting rubber my only warning.

Neighbors lift their noses as they smell our wood-pile, scanning the horizon as they look for the line of smoke filling the sky, wondering what's burning. Black, dark smoke, the telltale sign of an oil-based fire. But the gray, almost white column identifies a farmer's fire. A cluster of columns usually means an entire orchard or vineyard is burning—a farmer has pulled and piled something old while making way for something new.

What began as a huge pile early in a day ends with ashes. I don't believe you felt powerful with each burn; you didn't work as a conqueror laying your victims to waste. We renew the farm with each fire while reducing the pile to nothing. At the end of the day, we trudge home, worn out, but the pile is reduced to ashes, the embers burning all night.

Later, at home, I realize how smoky we smell. The scent penetrates all our clothes, even our hair. We shower and wash our clothes and still the smoke remains, embedded in the fabric, and for weeks we relive the autumn burn pile, accompanied by a faint scent of smoke.

Dad, you and I are about the same size. Years ago, when I lived with you, we occasionally got our clothes mixed up. As I buttoned a work shirt, I thought it smelled old, with a hint of your sweat but still clean. Now, at near eighty years old, you have lost weight and slouch as you shuffle along; you no longer need all your work clothes. You gave them to me and even after laundering, I can't wash out your scent—nor do I want to.

Your son,
Mas

MAY

# Lizard Dance

Dear Baachan,

Out on the farm it's fairly common for critters to
crawl into your clothes and fly into body cavities.
You never seemed to be afraid of them or make
much of a fuss.

"*Mushi*," you called them, shaking your shirtsleeves
to free a grasshopper or rubbing your eyes to tearfully
wash out a leafhopper. It took me a while to figure
out that *mushi* meant insect in Japanese. I thought
you were teasing us kids by announcing "mushy"
before squishing a captured bug in your hand. I
remember squirming as you held a bulbous tomato
worm, whispered *mushi*, and squeezed it like a tube of
green toothpaste.

You taught me not to be bothered by these bugs and to treat them as occasional visitors. Like the time a gnat zoomed into my ear, its wings fluttered as it penetrated deeper, hopelessly lost in the darkness near my eardrum, the pounding and wild beating. Yes, I knew it was just a gnat, but panic swept my thoughts; my heart raced, and my chest heaved as the frantic creature convulsed.

The solution was simply to tilt my head to the sunlight, hoping the bug would follow the warmth and light to freedom. It required the patience that you seemed to have. You'd stand calmly and collect yourself, waiting for the visitor to check out.

We share this land with creatures seen and unseen. We all belong—part of the life you found here in America. After all, who was here first, the critters or us? Are we not the invaders pretending to be conquerors in this new land? Yet as an immigrant, you thought differently: There was plenty of space for all to share.

Critters teach me about surrounding life, as we try to fool ourselves into thinking we can keep all creatures out of our homes and work. The bugs of the world help us understand that we don't live in a sterile world, nor would we want to. Besides, total control is fiction.

Still, I don't need to share all my space with every red ant or mosquito. Paper wasps and their nasty stingers don't have to make their homes under the eaves of our farmhouse or in the canopies of grapevines. I'm guilty of becoming selective about my visitors.

Baachan, I regret not knowing which *mushi* were your guests and which you didn't tolerate. It would have told me much about you, your childhood on a farm in Japan and your years of struggle here in California as an alien. To know someone's tolerance of critters and creatures is to understand that person's individual story, the history of a family and the places it has called home.

You knew scorpions well, for example, from the relocation camps in the Arizona desert during World War II. You shook your clothes before putting them on. (Mom told me about the showering facilities and how scorpions liked to hide in the pile of clothes waiting to be put on.) I understand Gila monsters were the other native residents, warranting a quick check of beds before crawling under a blanket. These stories help me understand that you were the visitors in this desolate land; I imagine you hoped daily that your stay would be brief.

And the stories stimulate my memory. I remember the day I felt something repeatedly brush my leg while I was shoveling weeds. Finally, I shook my leg and the thing bolted upward. I threw down my shovel and stamped my feet, my heart racing as I initiated my lizard dance. I patted my pants as the poor creature ran wild up my leg, but the faster I twisted and turned, the more confused the lizard became as he scrambled up and down the dark caverns of my pants.

My body danced uncontrollably to the feel of its tiny feet and little claws grabbing my skin. I tried to slow down, knowing the lizard would as well, if we both just relaxed. But as the creature scampered up higher and higher, my imagination ran wild; vulnerable body parts flashed in my mind.

I frantically tried to drop my pants. With luck, I would not open a crevice in my shorts, inviting the lizard into yet another dark hiding place. Instead, my visitor was attracted to daylight, leaped out of my crotch and tumbled to the ground before scampering into the safety of weeds.

Baachan, you too had your lizard dances. *Mushi* and crawling creatures belonged in the fields, along with the visitors who worked the land. Dropping our pants was all part of working with nature and our personal tales. We didn't plan on raising gnats or lizards but they're as much a part of the natural farm landscape as workers, family and farmers.

I once told my lizard tale to a new friend who then shared a story about her father, a farmer who was working with his farm foreman. A lizard had danced up the farmer's leg but the old timer had managed to trap it near his pants pocket. Clamping both hands over the squirming creature, he tried to keep it from scampering any more. He turned to his foreman and said, "Quick, unzip me!"

Now that's the ultimate test of loyalty in the fields and a story full of life.

Mas

# Hunger for Memory

Dear Dad,

You taught me to have a hunger for memory. Not nostalgia and a longing for the past that can never again be, but memory that's alive with a passion for excellence.

Such is the simple memory of eating a wonderful peach. First your eyes detect a subtle glow. "Background color," farmers call it; an amber radiance as the early morning sunlight is captured in the fuzz. Translucent.

Raise to the mouth and an aroma enchants, stirring anticipation. Insert in mouth and bite: juices splash and squirt, then drip down the cheeks and dangle on the chin. Flavors explode and the nectar dances across the taste buds. Swallow, and an aftertaste lingers and stays. You smack your lips and then pause before another bite, savoring the moment—slowly.

You helped me remember all this by keeping a peach with flavor while the marketplace laughed at the farmer with his yellow-skinned peaches with pointy tips. By the 1980s buyers were rewarding fruits with good looks: lipstick-red color and hard bodies. We lost money most of that decade, our cosmetically challenged produce selling at a lower price.

Our family farm was never about trying to make it big with piles of money, though. Instead, you instilled a desire to create a memory of something great and the passion to rediscover it each summer. I inherited your quest to keep that flavor ripening each year.

So I continue to walk through the peach orchard like you did, searching for perfection. Early morning is the best time; the ripening fruit glows, the light captured in peach fuzz, the sun alive in each piece. After years on the farm, I know where the earliest maturing branches are. I pick only the best and bring them home to share with the family. We stand around the butcher-block island in the kitchen, salivating as the first great peach of the year is sliced, shared and savored.

I think of our peaches as art and want them to tell a story worth remembering: How we planted one orchard thirty years ago, lining up trees by sight—most rows straight, a few trees slightly crooked. I must have planted those. I'm reminded of them at each pass through the fields on the tractor, swinging wide around my mistakes.

I think of your life's work as a priceless gift you passed on to another generation, a different sort of legacy that parents hope to leave behind, measured neither in wealth nor land but a portfolio of stories.

Dad, your spirit for perfection goes beyond our farm's boundaries. Great fruits work with a memory economy—consumers driven by desire anchored in memories of flavor. It seems that mass-produced produce is designed to excite only the visual sense, but biting into a memorable fruit becomes a journey into taste, texture and aroma. Personalized produce is what artisan farmers strive to grow. A family farm signature travels with each piece of fruit.

A great peach can transport us to someplace else: the memory of a tree in a grandpa's backyard; thoughts of mothers and daughters in summer kitchens canning peaches or making jam; summer visits to a farm where we lost our peach virginity and truly tasted flavor for the first time. These stories join our meals—wonderful foods that provide a social connection to places and people.

I fondly recall gorging myself as a child on juicy summer fruits. You'll remember that until I was a teenager, I was quite fat and all my white T-shirts had the same pinkish-red stain running down their fronts, arching toward the edge of a robust tummy.

After washing, then drying them on the clothesline, Mom would hold up a stained shirt in the sunlight. "Peach juice," she would say while shaking her head. She wasn't angry, because she knew that kids enjoying their family's fruits seemed like a good thing. I think of these stories when I eat—and never eat alone.

My greatest fear, though, is that there is a generation with no hunger for memory, that whatever they find in a typical grocery store is good enough. Who's going to demand a peach that they've never had?

Without memory, peaches become a commodity, consumers attracted by the cheap prices of fruit. Gone are the words that help commit experience to memory. We lack a language of taste, one of the main ingredients for creating lasting flavor and meaning. And when foods lack story, no one hears the farmer's voice. The person who grows our food is easily dismissed.

Dad, without knowing it, you taught me a lesson about how to save our farm. When we work as artisan farmers, we excite consumers with our spirited passion. It's OK to dream of perfection. The memory of a perfect food moment can become our greatest marketing tool. We all should hunger for memory.

Your son,
Dave Mas

# TWO

# Family Letters

I once wrote a list of things to say to my family before I die. The list was quickly divided into reflections to share with my wife, ideas to share with my children and impressions to tell my dad and mom while they were still alive. The best evolved into stories, thoughts put into context—gratitude to my grandparents and the weeds they battled in their lifetime, appreciation of the meals my mom prepared during the holidays. To my children I offered advice; words of counsel and not simply opinion. Written as letters to my family, these stories gain a public life—no longer a list of secrets we wish we had said, words we regret never sharing. I hope to leave behind family stories that bind.

# Spring Weeds

Dear Baachan,

Spring appears each year with the sudden green blanket of luscious weeds. You knew this well, nothing new for your calloused hands.

I remember you searching for your favorite shovel, stored in the barn since last fall. The one with the smooth handle well-oiled by your hands over the years, the shovel blade tip long ago worn away. Then, on the first warm day of the new year, in a single after-noon of work, you erased the brown tinge of winter rust from the shovel face, the steel gray and silver pol-ished by a thousand strokes in the soft moist earth.

The weeds lie in ambush all winter, gathering strength with each rainstorm and finally bursting, well, everywhere. They're good at disguising themselves:

initially as cute, slender shoots that paint the earth with a light emerald hue. Trick me into a smile as I stand in the sunshine, breathing in the start of a year, surrounded by new life. The sly weeds take advantage of my trance—delicate and innocent one day, a growing menace the next.

With the first shovel of spring earth turned over, Baachan, you shared a recognition with our valley's thousands of farmers and gardeners: the feel of something plowed back into the soul; breaking winter's crust to plant, water and tend the spirit. Begin the journey with weeds, a rite of passage, the ritual we call spring. We treat ourselves to a glorious moment, even if in denial—after all, aren't weeds part of the good earth too?

Did you ever think of yourself as a weed, an alien to this Valley, a foreigner who may not have always felt welcomed? You and Jiichan (Grandpa) could not own land, because of a racist law preventing "Orientals" from buying land while others—from Germany, Sweden, Italy—planted roots in American soil. (When Jiichan arrived in 1899, his Armenian neighbors were classified as "Asiatics," but when you came as a picture bride in 1918, authorities had already ruled Armenians were Caucasian and could become landowners, while Japanese Americans were exiled to work these fields.) Then, despite the upheaval of World War II relocation exiling all the Japanese Americans from the West Coast, you came back to this Valley to weed.

Along with tending vineyards and orchards, you and Jiichan grew a family and found a niche in this Valley. Accept, adapt, adopt: you survived because you became native to a place. I'm inspired. Tenacious, stubborn, persistent. Like weeds?

A philosopher/gardener once proclaimed that a weed was simply a plant whose virtues we had yet to discover. A weed was just something growing in the wrong place at the wrong time. I'd like to see that philosopher's farm: morning glory choking peach tree's roots, foxtail drinking up irrigation water and pigweed gorging itself in the shade of an anemic vine. It would probably drive you and me crazy.

Yet perhaps there's some truth in it: Not all things foreign to a field are weeds. (A convenient rationalization since I've given up trying to dominate all that's growing on our farm). The trick you taught me is to redefine what I call a weed.

A neighbor calls his: "native grasses." I like that term. Not as evil as weeds. Acknowledges that most of us here (like the vast majority of our weeds) came from somewhere else and forged a place in this soil. With the magic of time, we became natives, calling this land home as if we too would always be here, just as the weeds would always be with us.

So now I learn their proper names. Shepherd's purse blooms near Valentine's Day and has tiny heart-shaped leaves. Chickweeds have a miniature white flower, the first blossoms of a new year. Even fiddle-necks, mostly tolerable because they will dry out by the middle of summer. Someone once asked if I planted those colorful wildflowers. Wild to think my weeds become someone's flowers.

Naming weeds adds life to our fields. I laughed at myself after Marcy convinced me to plant Queen Anne's lace in our flowerbed and a visitor from the East Coast could not believe we actually planted weeds that flourish along eastern roadsides. Or when I read that dandelions were first prized as salad greens. Or recalled an old neighbor who came by to harvest our purslane; he claimed it was wonderful to eat as a salad. A step up, perhaps, from dandelions?

Baachan, you knew weeds better than most of us because you hand-shoveled them all. You understood that all farmers and gardeners struggle with some of them—despite their hidden virtues—because we also try to grow other things. Peaches and raisins put food on the table, not lamb's quarters or mare's tails.

You had a special name for some weeds; you called them *abunai kusa*, which in Japanese means "dangerous grass." You called johnsongrass and Bermuda grass dangerous because they can choke a tree's root system and shade out a grapevine. You did not tolerate puncture vines and sandbur and neither did the raisin inspectors. These weeds were dangerous because they could truly harm a farm.

But your secret was teaching which weeds we can also live with. Life is too short to worry about them. Now I am learning to recognize the weeds in my life, and which are indeed *abunai kusa*.

Mas

AUGUST

# The T-Shirt Scale

Dear City Cousins,

I'm not sure you understand sweat.

Out on the farm, I've tasted sweat: the salty, tangy flavor that drips down my temples, slides across my cheeks and beads on my upper lip. Sweat has stung my eyes, burning and blinding; I blink and it stings even more, forces me to work slow or stop, waiting for tears to wash my sight clean.

When I sweat, my T-shirts and work shirts are the first articles of clothing soaked, followed by hats and gloves, and of course underwear and socks. A few days will burn so hot even my leather belt is stained. Only the belt loops of my pants have never been saturated.

Sweat defines the character of this valley I call home. We euphemistically call our summer weather "dry heat" as temperatures rocket to 100 and 110 degrees, usually with little humidity.

I think of Valley sweat as clean and honest, not the sticky feel of the American South, with high humidity that gradually sucks energy out of me. I grow weary in such muggy weather. Valley heat quickly drains me, but enough liquids replenish me.

It's not the cool summer sweat of the Midwest, which sends a chill across my damp chest and confuses my senses. When I sweat, I like to believe it's 100 degrees. Nor is it the sweat of big cities, where you feel the grime penetrate your lungs and coat your skin. Rub my arms with fingers and create a smudge, a blend of smog, soot and perspiration—on bad days I can make little dark "snakes" of sweat and city dirt on my skin. It's easy.

But those of us who labor outside work hard. I identify with others, in construction or road crews, for example, in the middle of a summer afternoon. Hot, hot days that bond us laborers. We want to start with the first sunlight at 5:30 to avoid some of the heat and beat the sweat.

We wear universal badges of honor, work shirts darkened with moisture and, later, deposits of white blotches under our armpits or across our chests in a V-shape. Our hats survive like the veteran baseball player's old, worn cap with sweat stains on the brim. We wear these to tell the world we work "out there" in the blast furnace of the outside world.

I suppose sweat is sweat, even if resulting from exercise gyms. But that's self-inflicted sweat that can be stopped any time. Bottom line: it's not work.

Sweat is an involuntary reaction, heat the usual source. Yet even in an air-conditioned car, I've felt the rush of warm moisture break across my skin— generated by stress and nerves. Like the time I was driving fairly fast and suddenly a CHP officer appeared in my rearview mirror, accompanied by my utterance not for children. I think of this as perspiration and it doesn't count as sweat. As the cop cruised by, my heart slowed, I relaxed and stopped perspiring. Sweating doesn't stop that easily.

Sweating is the body releasing fluids to cool you down. Dogs don't sweat, they pant and hang their tongues out. Horses do sweat, that's why they're often wiped and brushed after a workout. "Sweat like a pig"? That expression is incorrect. Swine don't have the glands to sweat and thus have difficulty releasing heat. That's why they lie in the mud, wallowing in something cool to keep body temperatures low.

Humans respond to sweat differently. Many take the swine approach, preferring not to sweat and finding numerous ways to avoid hot situations and hide in air-conditioned buildings. (In the 1920s Fresno unveiled one of the nation's first air-conditioned buildings.) Others use powders and chemicals (read: deodorants) which block or mask our sweat, keeping the appearance of dry armpits and chests, cloaking the smell of body aromas.

I consider myself a master of sweat, first learning how I perspire. I'm a chest-wetter and beads of sweat on my forehead appear only later during the extremely hot stages. And I have studied how to live with sweat. I used to stay in the same work clothes throughout the day. After all, why change when I'll just sweat more in the afternoon and evening? But I've found I can renew energy by changing my T-shirts often. During that annual run of consecutive 105-degree days, I'll change my shirts three to four times, draping them over the farmhouse porch rail to dry stiff in the sun. Marcy, my wife, can drive into our yard at the end of her workday, glance at the rail, and count the shirts to determine how hard a day I've had.

Changing shirts allows me to take breaks, tricking myself into thinking I'm refreshed and can go right back out there. Actually it's my method to pace myself, recognize the fact that work has to be done no matter the temperature and accept the reality that I will sweat some more.

I think the weather reports should forecast a sweat index using my T-shirt count. A hot day is a one- or two-shirt day, very hot may be a three-shirt day, and a killer heat wave demands four or more. I ran out of shirts on the worst day this summer and was forced to recycle one from the morning. It felt dry but the aroma told me something else.

There are two categories of people who sweat: those that complain and those that accept it as part of work. The whiners want to control nature, fixing the heat with air conditioning and promoting the fallacy that we are masters over nature. Those who seem not to mind know the work that needs to be done. (We often lie, convincing ourselves it could be worse as we trudge back outside for more abuse.)

Farmers may be the best examples of the latter. Harvest time often comes with heat (that's how plants usually work) and we have no choice; fields need to be watered, weeds shoveled or peaches and grapes picked. Ask farmers if they can get work done despite the heat. With a slight nod, perhaps an impish grin (they know they're lying), they'll answer: "No sweat."

Your country cousin,
Mas

# Holiday Meals

Dear Mom,

I know you tried your best to provide us with traditional holiday meals. You found recipes for glazed ham and stuffed turkey, candied yams and pumpkin pie. And, of course, you added a big can of applesauce for the ham and a huge bowl of cranberries for the turkey.

But Dad wanted white rice with his meats and Baachan still brewed green tea for our holiday toast. We also grew confused with the applesauce and cranberries; we treated fruits as desserts and never ate them as a condiment. We knew what a holiday table was supposed to look like, but no one told us how it was supposed to be eaten.

Mom, you were a Nisei (second generation of Japanese in America). And possibly because of your treatment as an alien and the enemy during the World War II relocation of all Japanese Americans, you so desperately wanted to be a good citizen. Preparing the proper holiday meal was one step in becoming American.

Ironically, while growing up I longed for a taste of something else. Gravy and mashed potatoes didn't seem to belong among our family's simple recipes from the rural villages of Japan. Yet later, when I journeyed to Japan to sample its culture, I remember waking up one Christmas morning, eating a cold sunny-side-up egg (Japanese, too, knew what a Western breakfast was supposed to look like), then riding a train to school. I was a college exchange student in Tokyo, and at the end of the day, on the return train ride home, some passengers and I had bought a Kurisumasu keeki (Christmas cake). It felt strange and wrong as we rode in silence, the little decorated boxes of a dry white cake bouncing on our laps. I then realized the holiday tastes I longed for were not in Japan.

I sought the authentic taste of Japanese Americans, a fusion of two worlds and two palates: I wanted turkey dressing we ate with hashi (chopsticks) and a green lettuce salad with shoyu (soy sauce) dressing. Traditions can be lively and evolving, not a nostalgic memorial to the past. Behind the foods of a holiday table lie stories to be passed down, mixed and kneaded, stirred and whipped, baked and presented to a new generation.

At our Japanese New Year's celebration, for example, we offer a serving of salmon to honor the gathering of family; salmon is a fish that returns to its birthplace. But I enjoy salmon smoked with authentic mesquite wood, and some of the best were from Alaska and Washington. Or the tradition at our table, for family celebrations, of serving herring, the one fish with more eggs than any other, to symbolize fertility and long life. The herring I like, though, is more German and Midwestern, discovered during a holiday trip to Marcy's family in Wisconsin, where convenient, small jars of pickled herring in a white sauce are very popular and common.

Marcy's family from Wisconsin also had its holiday menus. Much to my delight, they used raisins in stollen pastries and even in turkey stuffing. Finally, a Japanese American Buddhist raisin farmer found a way to fit into the cheese lands of Wisconsin German Lutheran or Catholic households. And for some reason, her family often made oyster stew part of a Christmas Eve meal. Oysters didn't exactly fit my image of Midwestern German cuisine. Still, I had an

Asian affinity for seafood, so when the son-in-law asked for seconds—and even thirds—Marcy's mom beamed proudly. Traditions have an odd way of contributing to a feeling of acceptance.

I wonder how other cultures have maintained holiday traditions. I know the tradition of making tamales continues in many Mexican families. But I wonder, are men now invited into some kitchens, and do non-Hispanic family members participate? I know of a Greek holiday bread called *vasilopita* which is baked with a gold or silver coin kneaded into the dough. Then, at the family New Year's Day gathering, the bread is cut and whoever gets the slice with the coin will have good luck the entire year. Is a younger generation learning of this family recipe for good fortune?

In the future, could we in the Valley create our own fusion holiday foods? Could there be a sarma sushi, steamed rice rolled in grape leaves for the annual blessing of the grapes? Or perhaps the opposite, a sarma filling wrapped in nori (seaweed) for a New Year's Day feast? A Southeast Asian spring roll with masa and cornhusks for Christmas? The flavors of our valley can simmer and stew together into a delicate and seasoned sauce or a rich and fattening dessert.

Holiday tables require us to pay attention and make ourselves available for a culinary journey. The trick is to eat slow, savor the flavors of culture and ask questions, enjoying the stories behind the foods on our tables.

Thanks, Mom, for your holiday meals and stories that will be savored for generations.

Gochisosama!
Bon appetit!
Kali orexi!
Đố ăn ngon quá
Paree akhorjhag!
¡Panza llena corazón contento!
Nrog peb noj mov!
Das schmeckt gut!

Mas

  *Author note: What's your favorite traditional holiday food? I'm starting an informal collection. Let me know at masumotobee@aol.com.*

MARCH

# Big Fat Envelopes

Dear Nikiko,

Sometime this month or the next, my daughter, I hope you'll be getting a fat envelope from college. Inside lies your acceptance letter, the package made fatter with registration papers, housing information and other materials for the future student. A skinny envelope is not good, the single-page letter of rejection.

I can imagine the moment: A letter sits on the counter as you pause and take a deep breath; you might walk away—excited, nervous, fearful—then return and slowly pick it up. Doubt flashes in your mind. The envelope is not heavy. Panic surges, your stomach tightens. Or does it feel fat, could it be? You bargain, whispering, "Please, please, please."

Are you going to be a "tearer" and rip open the letter with your fingers? Or the "controller," seemingly calm, projecting an it's-not-that-important demeanor on the outside while shaking on the inside as you use a letter opener to slit the flap and slowly unveil the contents. These emotions are all doubled for parents, who may see the letter before you, be tempted to open it ourselves or call you for permission to "do it for you," as if doing you a favor.

Envelope opened, your eyes scan for the word "congratulations," and with a leap in the air you scream and grin, pump a fist up and down and howl, "Yes!" I would understand, though, your disappointment should you see the phrase "Due to the large number of highly qualified..." Disappointment, but not failure.

For a while you may feel sad, even angry. Please realize you took a risk and that's good. I sometimes wonder if we're overprotective at times, fearing failure so much that we avoid taking chances. Remember that in the long term, with most anything in life, risk will be rewarded.

Parents often live vicariously through fat envelopes—education as a means for bettering a family, a tool of class mobility. We encourage our children to improve themselves and then we share in your excitement of opportunity.

If we harbored any regrets in life, college offers redemption: we hope our children don't make the same mistakes. In a bittersweet way, part of me hopes you'll get off the farm, as I shake my head at the hard work ahead and the growing challenges. Is there much value in my work? Yet another part dreams of your getting the education you seek and somehow coming back home, even if only during harvests, as we redefine the meaning of a new family farm. I pass on the wisdom of my father and your *jiichan*: by giving me the opportunity to leave, he also opened the door to come home again. I do the same.

For many parents, a child going to college is a family decision. Private colleges can cost $35,000 to $40,000 a year, with a University of California or state university campus in California running $10,000 to $15,000. That's $40,000 to $160,000 for your degree, so it's neither an easy nor simple decision.

But it is true: education is an investment. According to federal statistics, with no high school diploma you'll earn an average $22,000 a year. With a high school education, that increases to $30,000. But you will be further rewarded for going to college. Annual income with a bachelor's degree should leap to $55,000; a yearly bonus of $25,000 can come with that fat envelope.

Fat envelopes mean more than just money. Some of our best and brightest youth will leave the Valley, longing for something on the "other side of the mountains." I recall applying for a UC Berkeley scholarship thirty years ago, a farm boy thinking he was ready for the big city. During my interview I described family life on the farm and explained that even my "big-city cousins" came to help with harvest during the summers. The interview panel asked which large city I meant: "San Francisco or Los Angeles?" I proudly blurted, "Fresno!" and was greeted with smiles and some laughter. I hungered for life someplace else.

For rural communities, whose children could stay in the Valley and attend a local institution, a brain drain can take some of our gifted native sons and daughters away from places that may need them the most. But it's wrong to shelter children and limit their imagination. We should expect and encourage them to go to college, wherever that may be, aware that the slightest hesitation can create doubt. Without absolute support, too often our youth self-destruct and adopt a fatalistic attitude, constructing obstacles that erode ambition. For your high school friends, today should never be as good as it gets.

I've seen that in some of your friends. Back in middle school they seemed to have ambition, but now, suddenly, life is limited. Talk of college quickly translated into excuses about perceived barriers and challenges too great to overcome. Some may be real, but many are myths: Consider that in the Valley, only one in four of those eligible even apply for California grant aid, money that could offset major college expenses. So they go to school close to home instead of chasing a dream or, worse, don't go to college.

The problem may be that fat envelopes aren't anticipated enough. This is all about opportunity, and getting that acceptance letter is one of the few moments in your life where paths diverge, a true fork in the road. Certainly, college is not necessarily right for every student, but I'm talking about giving you the chance to make that choice.

I hope you get many fat envelopes. And I hope this will be the first of many fat decisions you'll be making in your life.

Best of luck,
Dad

RANCH
FOR SALE
by owner
74± ACRES THOMPSON VINEYARD

# Advice to Farm Kids

Dear Nikiko and Korio,

Children, your grandparents grew up during the Great Depression, when the economy imploded and hard times lingered for more than a decade. Now I understand what that was like. On the farm, however, the current collapse didn't simply begin one day like the stock-market crash in October 1929. For the past two years, a gnawing depression has been slowly sucking life from me, a little each month and season.

I began this year knowing there was a huge surplus of grapes and raisins. Even as the crop grew to record size, I had no idea it would be this bad—a harvest no one wants.

Once prices for wine and juice grapes were announced, dreams of profits quickly faded. I penciled out our losses and realized a year's worth of labor had been wasted, nothing gained. Now, after weeks of crawling on my knees, working with a worthless raisin crop (already there's talk about hundreds of tons of raisins being used as cheap cattle feed), I have concluded we would have been better off not growing a single berry and letting the vines go wild. Grapes of wrath, 2002.

There's no single person or event to blame for this, just too many grapes and what I fear the most: just too many farmers. Times like this, I hear voices from the past that offer unsolicited advice like a haunting echo, questioning my choice to come back to the farm.

*Farming is too risky. Unpredictable. You can't bank on anything.*

I knew we'd never make lots of money farming, but that's not why I returned to the family farm. A neighbor once told me, You'll be land rich but always cash poor. Your mom and I were naive; we accepted that fact and still believed we could live a good life. And we have. But a year like this one makes me worry about the future.

*It's hard, dirty work that no one else wants to do. A life of poverty.*

I tried to adjust with the changing times and demands to boost production, cut expenses and become efficient. Be lean; be mean. Now we have more grapes, lower prices and a bleak outlook on the horizon. For the family farmer, production agriculture no longer works.

*Escape while you can. The farm will drain you. There's no future in farming.*

What does it mean when a father tells his children not to follow him? Is my work worthless? I joke about knowing how to increase our wealth: pull out our grapes.

Meanwhile, down the street the "For Sale" signs sprout

like evil weeds and tell a shocking story of losing neighbors I had expected to be with for a lifetime.

*The work is isolating. Monotonous and lonely.*

Yet when I'm by myself I can find those moments of pleasure: a sunrise reflected in a golden peach or the scent of drying raisins during early autumn evenings. As I prune our peaches, I can't help but envision the tree's shape for years to come. I still talk with grapevines as if they were old, dear friends.

*Someone has to grow our food. Learn to work with nature. Purge the negatives.*

Like a fool, I'll go out to work today and tomorrow. That's what farmers do. My spirit may be broken this season, but with farming there's always more work to do. After all, I've heard that hope is the last to die—and that following winter comes spring.

*Work as a craftsman, sweat as an artisan. The art of farming keeps you going.*

If we survive, the new family farm of your generation will look very different. You'll add off-farm income and welcome the necessary complexity of financing, marketing and promotion to my simple legacy of growing a succulent peach, sweet raisin. You can then give me advice and harvest stories for another generation.

I end this letter with a sample of the twisted humor of farmers and their necessary optimism.

*They did an autopsy on an old farmer and when they opened him up, they found he was full of "next years."*

And a stubborn streak in me still believes there will be a next year.

Love,
Your dad

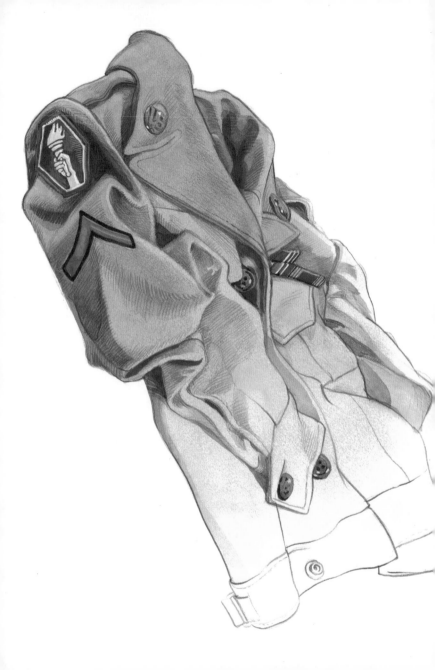

# Becoming a Soldier

Dear Uncle George,

You died October 16, 1944, in northeastern France, fighting in World War II, battling alongside other Japanese Americans of the 442nd Infantry Battalion. Were you a good soldier?

I never met you, born after that war, just a little too young to be drafted into Vietnam, an observer of the more recent confrontations with Iraq. While debating the politics of war, whether the United States belonged in the jungles of Asia or the deserts of the Middle East, a voice often has been whispering, asking the question: would I have become a good soldier?

Good soldiers follow orders and carry out commands. I wonder if I could have followed an order of "charge" or "advance forward" without a moment of hesitation that challenges authority? Are you trained not to think or do you simply not ask questions? Uncle, did you die because you carried out an order? Or was it because the life of the soldier next to you also depended on you—a deeper order that good soldiers understand?

Good soldiers develop skills to march, shoot, fight hand-to-hand, aim artillery. But how do you learn to kill? A veteran told me it's about self-discipline, like living with the sounds of war—bullets whizzing by, bombs exploding, the wounded crying. You find a way to get used to it, knowing you will never be the same; a little of you dies with each incident.

Do all good soldiers lead, or is that for the officers? What's the difference between an officer and an NCO (noncommissioned officer)? Leaders must work with an instinct to direct and inspire, the survival of the company or platoon paramount, knowing men and women under their command may die. Leadership that demands courage to make hard decisions with a deeply rooted loyalty and allegiance to the foot soldiers. Perhaps the real question is the difference between a good officer and one who's ineffective. Not that it makes much of a difference now, but I hope you died because of a good command.

You were a private, a grunt, a GI. You learned to cope with the little things, the sweat, pain, anger. Were you ever afraid? Good soldiers sometimes are, but they know fear is a poison in war. Did you learn to hide it, even on that battlefield in France?

Good soldiers believe in a cause, something larger than themselves. They learn to fight as family, depend on each other. Wasn't that one of the 442nd's mottos, "Leave no one behind"? Is that why WWII veterans often think of themselves as a band of brothers? When you died, did your company feel the death of a brother?

Good soldiers fight with duty and honor, an obligation to country. A military officer tried to explain, you become a "person of honor." Those seem like fuzzy words to me. Uncle, how did you cope with a duty to country while that country imprisoned your parents, brothers and sisters in a relocation camp behind barbed wire in the Arizona desert? Yet that's why you fought, to prove yourself, to show America what it means to be

American. Courage, integrity and dedication, perhaps something not understood until challenges are faced.

I did not serve in the military. I never had to answer such questions. I now wonder if I would have ever become a good soldier because I question things too much. Yet when you're younger, maybe you don't know any better and follow orders. Or perhaps I'm now old and jaded with a loss of spirit. Good soldiers don't question if war is right or wrong. One 442nd veteran told me, "You just make the best of it." Uncle, you made the best of it.

"War is hell," they say and I agree. Yet why do soldiers fight? Good soldiers find their own reasons, a sense of obligation to serve. "Live if you can, die if you must, but do so with honor," a captain explained. That only makes sense if you believe and that's what makes for a good soldier: a personal commitment.

A good soldier in anything—teaching, healing or growing food, becoming a doctor, minister or businessperson—is all about doing what's right and doing it well. Then the ultimate complement may be: you've become a good soldier.

Thanks, Uncle.

Your nephew,
Mas

# THREE

# Community Correspondence

A Nisei widow asked if I would write and present a eulogy for her late farmer husband. She convinced me by saying, "Every community needs a storyteller." I write letters to my neighbors to document, reflect and respond to issues and everyday life. I work to tell the truth with neighbors I hope to have for a lifetime; about places where people have long memories while facing a rapidly changing economy and growing diversity. These letters are meant to be read and passed on to children so they will remember our communities, our flaws and accomplishments, our histories and cultures. We are defined by our stories and leave behind gifts of words.

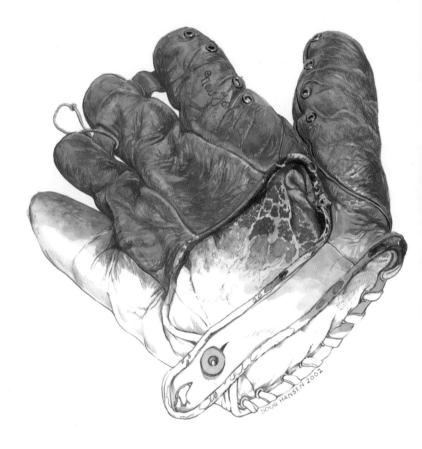

APRIL

# Baseball Saved Us

Dear Hiro,

Every spring with the first warm days and the smell of freshly cut grass, do you stretch your old legs, breathe in deeply and think of baseball?

You begin, my neighbor, with your own spring training, rising out of hibernation, working dormant muscles and stepping onto the field, rough dirt underfoot with hard sweat ahead. You move slow because that's the pace of early spring and baseball; a slow sport with no clock and games with no time limits. Plenty of moments to think. Like farming with the seasons, life stirs as we leave behind the cold, short days of winter and momentarily forget the approaching long, hot, grueling days of summer harvest. Baseball taught us to start anew, each year brimming with hope and optimism. It would be a few months before I'd have to

87

utter, "Wait till next year!" To some of us farmers, baseball saved us. But does it still fit today?

You played the game the way it was supposed to be played. A small five-foot, two-inch Nisei with speed and a quick bat. You talk of when you were drafted into the Army in 1941, and how during basic training the bombs fell on Pearl Harbor. The military didn't know what to do with you and other Japanese Americans—on the rifle range one day, treated like the enemy the next. While your families were rounded up and imprisoned in assembly centers at the Fresno fairgrounds, the Army confined you boys to the barracks and prohibited training with guns. What kind of soldiers could you be if you were never trusted?

Then, on a dusty spring day, you and a group of Nisei grew restless and challenged the other GIs to a game of baseball. The soldiers found you could play the American pastime even though at times you weren't treated like an American. You won that first game, lost one, won another. By the end things got better. All just boys playing a game. You claimed baseball saved you.

Baseball remains part of our community history: from the early days of the Fresno Athletic Club of Nisei ballplayers to Kenichi "Zeni" Zenimura building a baseball diamond in the desert of Arizona, behind barbed wire in a desolate place called Gila River. Fact often grew into legend.

We created our own heroes—Johnny Nakagawa, George "Hats" Omachi and, of course, "Zeni"— alongside the giants Babe Ruth and Joe DiMaggio. I've often wondered if Joe saved the Italian American fishing fleet in San Francisco when World War II was declared and "all enemy aliens"—Japanese, Germans and Italians—were ordered to register.

Our dream of a baseball stadium in downtown Fresno is now becoming a reality. But this is about more than just sports. This is about business and economic development stirred with hope and a game, a city investing millions to bolster the local community. We're asking baseball to save us.

Call me naive, but let's move beyond all the talk and debate and just play ball. It's the game that will save us in the end, clean fielding mixed with clutch hitting, a stolen base or well-executed bunt, and the one mighty swing of the bat that can determine the outcome of a game.

I grew up listening to baseball, working on the farm too much to play, but carrying a transistor radio, the kind that fits into your work-shirt pocket, listening to the voice of Vin Scully or Jon Miller recreating the game with words. Then I'd relive the game through the next day's *Fresno Bee* and the box scores. Baseball saved us farm kids.

My family didn't play ball like yours did, Hiro. We weren't gifted athletes and I never had a magical father-son moment playing catch. My children are not as connected to baseball and, in some ways, I'm glad. Youth sports have mutated into something else, highly competitive with well-meaning but overzealous and obnoxious adults who believe they have license to yell and scream and hurt. Thousands of dollars are now spent for youth club teams, traveling squads and private coaches. Success becomes solely defined as winning. Hiro, what if you had lost that first game against the other GIs?

I imagine, though, on that spring afternoon in 1942 you told the world something: We can play this game. You understood the power of the moment; to enjoy the sight of the ball soaring into the sky, rocketing to the heavens, and the artistry of a player sliding into second just under a tag. It's not about beating anyone, rather playing with style; a pitcher's release with a dare to "hit this heater" and the smooth, effortless swing as the answer.

Every spring I think of baseball and stories. His name was Jerry and we called him "Pops," an old man in his late thirties while we all were in our twenties. Like you, Hiro, he was a veteran. Jerry had served in Vietnam, and he brought to our young team something from a different generation.

The bases were loaded when he came to bat. The opposing outfielders moved in when they saw, stepping to the plate, a middle-aged, slightly saggy batter in a simple white T-shirt.

Jerry had other things on his mind. The Iranian hostage crisis was ongoing in 1980, with seemingly no simple answers. Earlier that day we had learned of the tragically aborted helicopter rescue and eight soldiers who had perished in the desert sandstorm, half a world from our baseball game. Jerry was quiet that day, like the way you, Hiro, must have often played.

He smashed a shot; the ball sailed into the air, climbing as the outfielders turned to stone. Later Jerry told us he did it for those soldiers who sacrificed their lives for us, fighting to protect and save all the good we have. So we could play baseball.

In a single swing Jerry told us that anything worth doing must be done right: a simple truth beyond our different colors of skin or social class, things a private coach could never teach. It's the hope a new stadium helps create for a city trying to believe in itself. Character in whatever we do, in whatever game we play, is worth our trying.

That's what I imagine you think of every spring and what I believe Jerry was thinking as he rounded third and ran for home to our cheers. As we too headed home.

Mas

# Old Friends

Dear Pam,

Will you come to my funeral?

I know we're much too young to be talking about death but this letter is really about friendship. We grew up as neighbors and our childhood years stretched across a horizon that seemed endless. Contrast that with the fast world we now live in, where relationships come and go and people move on so effortlessly with new work and homes.

Friendship has a slower pace, an accrual of memories over time and shared moments. People underestimate the value of staying put and planting roots.

We still see each other occasionally and when we meet I feel an initial embarrassment because we don't keep in touch as much as we should. You manage to bridge the uneasy silence with a smile that forgives as we slip into a comfortable conversation acknowledging the distance.

We have begun our own families, and watched our children grow and head off to college and their own lives. Do you ever feel we're left behind? We have witnessed dear friends leave, helping them pack and move, waving good-bye and knowing it will never be the same without face-to-face exchanges. As they depart for new adventures, do we simply stay here to grow old?

But then a warm feeling begins inside. The initial envy of life beyond the mountains transforms into a type of security blanket: We know who we are because we know where we are. We have a sense of place here in the Valley, a sense of belonging to a piece of land with a history we know well.

We are Valley folk, landed people who stay put, a true rarity these days. We both now have addresses that will probably stay the same for the rest of our lives. We remain part of farm families who know where home is.

We grew up a half mile from each other on neighboring farms. Our brothers and sisters were classmates and played as friends. We shared thirteen years of school, beginning in a small class of kindergartners, posing for black-and-white elementary school class pictures, and then signing the same high school yearbooks.

Your family moved once to a farm down the street, still along the same country road that somehow kept us linked. And then our family bought your farm. I now live with my wife and children in your old house, the place you grew up in, home to yet another farm family. As your mother says, that somehow seems all right, "how it should be."

I remember once finding an old, long, iron bar in the corner of the red barn, a heavy, five-foot metal pipe with a solid tip at the base. We used it to loosen and break apart chunks of hardpan scattered in our fields, those underground rocks that stood guard against change and a new orchard or irrigation line.

Curious about the origins of this tool, I visited with your father, who told me of its history. Workers had used it to set iron tracks and straighten rails before the metal spikes were pounded in.

"Could have even been a Chinese railroad laborer," your father explained. I felt a new affinity, sharing an Asian American working-class history in this heavy, iron bar. Your family provided the connecting story, the bridge between the past and present.

I feel a special sense of continuity so rare these days, not just a virtual connection via email or phone calls to keep in touch. I work the vines your father planted, walk the dirt avenues your family knew well and, on hot summer days, drink cool pump water from the same barnyard faucets. I can run my fingers along wooden floors in the living room that generations of farm kids learned to walk on. I can find your names in cement along walkways and barn floors. We, too, have left our handprints in fresh cement when we added a room to the farmhouse, leaving behind a little of our history.

We are getting older, and at near fifty, I hope I now have the wisdom to no longer judge others by their accumulation of material goods but rather by their acts. Things that matter.

This all seems amplified by these troubled times. But for us in agriculture, the depression in the farm economy tears at our hearts. We both see farmers hurting. Things that seemed eternal and forever— such as a farm neighbor—are quickly changing. "For Sale" signs announce trouble. I respond with my own list of things worth saving, things worth savoring. Friendships seem even more important.

So I ask in advance, Will you come to my funeral? I know what your answer will be, and I will do my best to do the same should you pass before me.

I'm not sure why this is important; perhaps it's just somehow comforting to know. Over and over, I fondly recall the last time we saw each other, our visit ending with a long hug and your whisper: "We will always be friends."

Your friend always,
Dave Mas

MAY

# Hardpan

Dear Dad,

    I think they should proclaim hardpan the official rock of the Valley. Hardpan, a compressed layer of clay that behaves more like a rock than dirt. Hardpan, lacking the nobility of granite or the texture of flagstone, a rather dull, tan chunk of parched earth that looks like all life has been squeezed out of it. Hardpan, hiding a few feet beneath the surface, shocking unsuspecting farmers, gardeners or even builders who try to work the land, growing crops or planting foundations, only to suddenly discover that shovels are worthless, pickaxes and sledgehammers more appropriate, backhoes and dynamite the best.

    Dad, you're an expert with hardpan, having spent years clearing it from our fields. Our land was initially cheap because of a hardpan discount. Half the place had fine Hanford sandy loam with vigorous vines and sweet peaches and plums already growing. The other half was barren and open. We quickly named it "The Hill"—a rise on the horizon hiding a mountain of stone, a shallow layer of hardpan protecting the virgin earth, frightening prior farmers and intimidating potential vineyards and orchards.

You spent two years clearing The Hill of hardpan. Called in a bulldozer to rip the soil and a sea of rocks that seemed to float in the earth like icebergs; tens of thousands of chunks you dragged, carried and heaved onto wagons and truck beds, hauling tons away, claiming this land as yours. Then, after another pass of the bulldozer, the seemingly clear field was blanketed again with more stones. Progress was measured by the pairs of leather gloves you wore through.

Most pieces were small, only ten to twenty pounds; others were thousand-pound flat sheets of hardpan that had to be broken with a hammer. In some spots even the bulldozer was unable to rip through the rock, the machine's claw bouncing over underground piles that seemed determined to fight relocation. You used dynamite to break the grip, shattering the stronghold, allowing a tractor shank to hook the remaining chunks and loosen them from their home. Mom shook with each blast, wondering who would get the best of the other: man versus rock.

I don't believe you saw it as winning or losing. All you wanted was to get a foothold here in this Valley, not to conquer and control but simply to plant a few vines and make a home. Now, a luscious vineyard stands on the hill. Occasionally, when a hardpan rock surfaces, we toss it along the ditch bank, where a wall of stone protects the bank from the swift currents, a reminder of staking a claim to this land.

Some may also designate hardpan as our valley's environmentally friendly rock. Indigenous to our lands, it has kept a few areas wild and unfarmed. Furthermore, with today's decline in farm value and poor crop prices, I've noticed that some of the first abandoned fields have uneven terrain and weak orchards and vineyards—signs of the influence of hardpan. Over the years, I predict these farms will revert back to their natural state, hardpan reclaiming her territory.

Hardpan, tough, not very pretty, a symbol of survival for immigrant families who came here to carve out a life for themselves. You don't work with hardpan if you're not planning on staying for a while.

Hardpan, a metaphor for the Valley. A rock that doesn't want to be moved, like the conservative politics of this place, where traditions become embedded, adaptation often slow, acceptance of difference difficult.

Hardpan was formed when this land was an ancient lake bed and the pressures of the water compressed the silt and mud. Likewise, it seems when political pressures from the outside challenge our way of thinking, we too hunker down and harden. Hardpan politics thrive here: people have long memories and distrust outsiders, often seeking local solutions to problems.

Are we out of synch with the rhythms of big-city America that seem to reward mobility and speed? Do hardpan politics allow us to adapt fast enough to the changing landscape? Our institutions—political, educational and social—are they still based on an antiquated system of people staying put and having a long-term stake in a place?

Or have we taken the right approach, building stable communities, waiting for the rest of the nation to come back to us and return to the conservative nature of hardpan politics?

Hardpan communities, the best of times and the worst of times. Local economies built on agrarian foundations and the constant economic struggle of low-paying, seasonal employment. Yet when outsiders accused you, Dad, of exploitation of farmworkers, you eloquently answered in a whisper, quiet yet powerful:

At least these hardpan farms created jobs for a people hungry for work.

When others measure our valley's worth by our poverty and social problems, they forget those of us who stayed put, planted roots and continue to hope for slow progress measured in a hardpan timeline of decades and generations. Some of us are as stubborn as rocks, embedded in a place we don't expect to leave. We then spend a lifetime trying to fix things and don't anticipate running away because of a low national survey ranking.

We continue to support public schools as most still do in our valley, accepting the good of our education system with the bad. We have many problems, and answers are often hard to come by. But our tolerance doesn't imply blindness. Perhaps you set an example for me, Dad, clearing our fields of rocks one by one, load after load, trusting that in the end we'd find a way to survive and even thrive.

Hardpan, a symbol of our rural past and a measure of our economic, social and political future. A slow lesson for our valley: Though we may be invisible at times, hiding just beneath the surface like hardpan, we're not going away.

Your son,
Dave Mas

# *Passion to Learn*

Dear Dan,

As a high school principal, have you ever considered starting the school year with a commencement speech? The promise of hope and inspiration in a few good words, a vision to look towards the future, commencement towards something more; messages that should begin the year instead of end it. So let me begin again.

Dear Dan and the Classes of 2004, 2005, 2006 and 2007,

Students in our valley too often have to apologize for being smart. Just as some kids are ashamed to be from a family farm or part of our rural landscape, those who are bright bear the burden of a valley-wide inferiority complex: kids sometimes have to hide their passion for learning.

Their thinking? Better to "dumb down" and offer excuses for mediocrity than be seen as having a hunger to learn, a thirst for knowledge. The passionate are often alone, isolated by their drive and enthusiasm. We lack a culture for achievement.

Consider the scene at a recent middle school graduation. As hundreds of young students marched in with pomp and circumstance, I glanced over to see a train of limousines lined up in the parking lot. Talk of huge parties filled the stands. All for eighth grade promotion?

A sage teacher shook her head. "For a third of these students, this is their last graduation. That's why the celebration and the limos. This is as good as it gets."

This is not just about those top kids with good grades and high test scores. For many from elementary to high school, it's not cool to be good at anything except, perhaps, sports. Better not to stand out. Instead try to fit in, finding company with dumb and dumber.

Dan, you were a former athlete and coach. What if academics were supported and promoted like sports? Imagine rallies, community interest, booster clubs for a U.S. history class, a pep rally with cheerleaders during the introduction of the starting lineup for the speech and debate teams. Hundreds gather as we send off biology students on their field trip, wishing them good luck in finding and identifying specimens.

In the fall before school starts, imagine students sweating two-a-day study sessions, preparing for the upcoming academic season. Local community talk fills lunch counters with a buzz about the chances for the band to win superior awards in competition. Families circle dates on calendars for the Advanced Placement (AP) tests in English, math and science.

"Only the Best" banners stretch across roads, a billboard greets us with a simple message: "Excellence." Some confident students even wear their motto on a button: "One day you'll be working for me."

With such a culture, education will be marketed differently. AP classes will be redefined: successful students will receive not only college credit in high school but a chance to save on college expenses. "Pass an AP test, earn hundreds of dollars." By my calculations, each class is worth $600 to $1,000, based on current expenses for college tuition. For students, it's like a summer job for every AP class passed. For parents, it's the perfect reward system.

A culture of achievement begins in elementary and middle schools, before "smart kids" are labeled. Every child hears the same messages repeatedly, not only at school but also in the community and at home: "You are expected to go to college." "You will continue on a course of lifelong learning." "Every student will find a way to succeed." Achievement works only within a broad culture of support; not lip service claiming support, but a commitment.

Dan, here are my suggestions, little gems based on real life, simple solutions we all have the power to effect.

First, at least on school nights, perform one of the hardest acts for many households, painful for *all* family members, demanding of the entire family: Turn off the TV, all the TVs.

I've imagined how to become one of the most unpopular parents in a community: sponsor a "No TV" school night and beg, push and demand for one class or one school to have 100 percent participation. We'd begin with a single night, then push for a few consecutive nights; the ultimate test may be Monday Night Football (what, no Raiders or Forty-niners?) or the conclusion of a reality TV show.

Second, ban video games, cell phones, phone calls, text messaging, instant messenger computer chat rooms, Internet surfing (unless for research, which really doesn't happen that much) and CD players on school nights. Don't answer phone calls; study time is sacred and not to be interrupted. The best concentration requires silence, a stillness that scares us at first. Imagine homes filled with an eerie quiet, so that when we speak, we actually listen to each other.

You will anger relatives, neighbors and friends when you don't instantly respond to their calls. Children will resent you for all the lost conversations, students will want to go over to friends' houses, supposedly to study, because your home is a prison. Keep them at home, cut out the distractions. Your children will hate you. And they will learn.

Third, sit next to your child as he or she studies. You don't need to help—much of their school material is already beyond me—just observe. We spend hours watching kids participate in sports, but rarely, if ever, watch them study. I've always believed most of learning is really just about thinking. Make time and a place to think, both of you.

Finally, like most good things in life, this all works better with passion. Imagine a Valley culture of achievement, driven by passion. It's OK to be smart, bright and good at what you do. Believe.

Mas Masumoto

# The Other California

Dear Nikiko,

After receiving numerous "fat envelopes" containing acceptance letters from colleges, you'll soon be running off to UC Berkeley. When you get there and people ask where you are from—a question many from the Valley have reckoned with—I wonder how you will respond.

Will you answer, "I'm from Del Rey," a phrase no one uses because Del Rey is so small it's not on most maps? Or do you simply respond "Fresno," generating responses about our dense winter fog and blistering summer heat? You may even speak of the "Central Valley" and begin to describe our rich farmland and connecting river of asphalt called Highway 99.

I suggest you say you're from "the other California."

The rest of the state and world often defines us by what we are not. Not Southern California with palm tree–lined streets, balmy weather, movie stars and freeways. (We really mean Los Angeles, and so we too are guilty of generalizing.) Not Northern California (probably thinking of San Francisco) and invigorating cool breezes, art, culture and haute cuisine.

Instead, we're the part of the state that becomes invisible, lost in between north and south, part of an inland desert that doesn't seem to belong.

While the economic boom of the Silicon Valley and Hollywood has evaded us, we still try to prove we're not just cows and crops, which, to some, represent a sixteen-billion-dollar embarrassment. Hidden from culture wars, we in the Valley tend to sit off to the side and shake our heads at the politics of the "left coast." We talk of our valley as being simply a good place to raise a family, more a part of Middle America than anywhere else and proud of it.

As outsiders move in, they're amazed at the cheap prices of land and housing; we welcome them and never test to see if they'll fit in here. We then let others change us, tearing up farms to make way for bedroom communities for the Bay Area, and we begin to believe their assessment: the other California is a region without an identity, the land of the indistinct and secluded, a place to pass through while venturing to someplace else.

We're an independent people, friendly and generous. You wave to strangers and expect a wave back; just enough of a Bubba syndrome we're comfortable with, but one which keeps outsiders thinking of us as, well, the other California. It's easy to neglect who we are, overwhelmed by what we are not.

Our valley teems with diversity. Consider the length of the Central Valley from Bakersfield to Chico; the ethnic and economic variation is just as diverse as a drive from San Diego to Eureka.

Should the big earthquake subtract the California coast and make our valley farmland into coastal property, our diversity will no longer be invisible. Imagine Chico as a reincarnated Mendocino, with Sacramento and Stockton becoming San Francisco, and Bakersfield our "SoCal." Then Fresno could be Monterey and we could fix the downtown area with a world-class aquarium. And Del Rey could become the new Carmel, with our farm part of the seventeen-mile drive. We stretch our creative imaginations from the other California.

OK, I accept being from the other California. We may never shine as brightly nor bloom as boldly as other parts of the state. Instead, Nikiko, I like to think of us as home to wildflowers from the other California.

Yes, wildflowers: natural flowers with a physical and geographic link to the land, regional in orientation, specific to a place. Others may consider wildflowers as weeds, a bias from the big city that you'll soon discover when you tell them where you're from.

But wildflowers are hardy plants; they adjust to changing conditions, demand little maintenance. They struggle to find niches in which to germinate and make homes in a broad range of conditions. They seem to have an independent soul, a quality of self-sufficiency.

You don't necessarily need to sow wildflower seeds. (Indeed, as a farmer neighbor astutely pointed out: "How can they be wildflowers if you planted them?") They spread in the winds and lie quiet and dormant for years, waiting to sprout with the proper conditions. They have learned from the rest of the world that there's power in mobility and in the ability to migrate and adapt.

So, my daughter, you are a wildflower, part of the natural beauty from a place mixed with a sense of the wild, in a valley that still feels rural, more country than big city. You are a simple gift from the other California.

Love,
Your dad

# The Good Neighbor

Dear Kamm,

You were a good farmer and a good neighbor and I will remember that forever. Before you passed away, we'd sometimes talk in the fields as our raisins dried, the scent of harvest in the air mixing with stories past and present.

September 1942: The same aroma of drying raisins, a caramel fragrance lingering in the vineyards of Fowler during a late summer evening. But that year, the bittersweet scent of history was in the air.

A year earlier Japan had bombed Pearl Harbor and America entered World War II. Quickly, Americans of Japanese descent were perceived as the enemy. During the spring of 1942, thousands of Japanese Americans living along the West Coast were ordered to move inland and placed in centers, including one in Pinedale and another at the Fresno fairgrounds.

Later, by the middle of summer, all Japanese Americans living in the western U.S. were exiled to relocation camps, banished to such desolate places as Tule Lake and Manzanar, California; Gila River, Arizona; and Jerome, Arkansas, all because they looked like the enemy. In August Japanese Americans in the Central Valley were forced to pack only what they could carry, sell what they could and leave behind everything else. Jobs were vacated, homes abandoned and, as school started in the fall, empty desks sat where once thousands of young Japanese Americans studied. They too were casualties of war.

But what happened to farmers? You couldn't take a harvest with you. In August the juicy grapes grew fat, but not ready for picking until the next month; a year's worth of labor invested, with a month to go before harvest.

The Masumotos then only rented land in the Selma area. Dad explained that we lost most of the crop, negotiating $25 a ton for a harvest that would eventually sell for $109 in 1942 and over $300 during the war years.

But, Kamm, you had a Japanese American neighbor, the Hiyama family, and knew them as friends. Over a handshake, you agreed to work their land "like it was yours," and all that September, Hiyama raisins dried in the sun as equals to yours. Some called you a "Jap lover" and you had some "back talk." I doubt if anyone called you what they should have: A good neighbor.

Later you simply said, "It was the right thing to do."

Yet it's often hard to stand up for what's right, to see others without labels and as neighbors. I've heard of a few other deeply personal stories, such as the Lotter family in the Bay Area. Mrs. Lotter was a music teacher with many talented Japanese American students who had to leave behind their pianos during evacuation. She found homes for these instruments with families who promised to play them often in order to keep the wood from growing hard and stiff. When Japanese American families returned after the war, they were reunited with their pianos and the music of good neighbors.

Then there's the story of Elaine Otomo (formerly Yoshino Uyemura) from Del Rey, who had to leave behind a new bicycle. Her father gave the bike to an Armenian family friend, the Blueians, and their daughter, Alice, who was Yoshino's schoolmate. Alice used it for years, her father all the while reminding her that the bike still belonged to Yoshino. Earlier this year, sixty years later, the burden was returned, bike

given back to its owner. These are private stories easily overlooked and forgotten. Too often they remained family secrets, as if it was wrong to publicize acts of good neighbors.

During internment Japanese Americans were shamed, losing property, belongings and respect. Good neighbors helped to maintain dignity despite the on-going tragedy. Now as these stories are shared publicly, they lift the human spirit and help the healing. People who are violated often cope privately, turning inward for the strength to survive. But internment publicly violated a people, and that demands a public forum—like stories—to serve as a type of public apology, a recognition that the Japanese Americans were not criminals but victims who were wronged. Kamm, you helped right the wrong with your personal act of courage.

For Japanese Americans and the Armenian Americans in our valley, September of 1942 added a twist, a bittersweet moment as family histories crossed paths. Some Armenian farm families saw a connection between the unfolding tragedy of internment and their own family histories involving the Armenian Genocide. Some Armenians insisted that their families take care of Japanese American farms. They knew what it was like to lose everything. Simple acts to insure history would not be repeated, at least between neighbors. For those Armenians, to close one's eyes to the present history was to deny their own tragic history.

That's why I'll think of good neighbors on this coming February 19th, an annual Day of Remembrance for Japanese American internment. On that day in 1942, President Roosevelt signed Executive Order 9066, beginning the process of uprooting and falsely imprisoning 120,000 Americans of Japanese descent.

And I'll also think of April 24th, the day of remembrance for the Armenian Genocide of 1915–1923. Good Armenian neighbors acted like you did, Kamm, ignoring the emotional hysteria fanned by politics and instead responding with a private act based on personal conviction.

Since the tragedy of September 11th, 2001, we've all recently been challenged to be good neighbors. Those who appear to be Arab or Muslim have sometimes been placed under suspicion, detained or attacked. I wonder how good of a neighbor I have been.

To be a neighbor is to know history and honor memories, not just the so-called "feel-good politics" of caring, but beliefs that operate on the personal level of doing what may not be popular.

I doubt if you, Kamm, stopped to think of your actions during September 1946 and whether they fit into some larger historical frame of race relations. You were about being a "Jap lover" and taking care of a neighbor's farm and their sweet raisins under a harvest sun. I'm proud to have later become your neighbor.

Thanks,
Mas Masumoto

*Author note: Do you have a story of Japanese American "good neighbors" during World War II? Let me know at masumotobee@aol.com.*

# *How to Write a Letter*

Dear Nikiko and Korio,

I have a dream, my children, that sometime in the future (a long, long time from now, I hope), as I grow very old and near my life's end, I will write you a letter, sharing what few lessons I've learned in life, passing on a bit of wisdom I have been fortunate to learn and leaving behind a piece of myself.

A piece of paper, my final hug with words; a letter that's meant to be read over and over, to be passed on and shared among family, friends and generations, not a conversation in which words can be forgotten and shared only secondhand.

I imagine the stacks of letters people have saved, an old habit I hope continues when people realize that even a few words can warm our memories and that stories are the important things we leave behind. My *baachan* saved a few. One was a telegram she sent my grandfather announcing her arrival in America: "Arrive Seattle Wednesday." That's the beginning of our family in America, a quiet and humble beginning. Three simple words reflecting the spirit of that first-generation immigrant.

Another was your mom's stack. I guess you could call them love letters, which I wrote to her, you know, during that young-love stage of infatuation. (Oh so romantic then, they seem silly now.) Letters speak volumes; they can be saved and relived. Try that with a phone call.

In my letters people matter, which is part of a letter's personal nature. I set the tone by beginning with the word "Dear," a serious word about caring, to be read slowly and with meaning. Then come your names, a final moment a father shares with his children. My letter to you will take time to compose, quality time because quality words require quality thought.

Letter writing is supposed to be slow. Good writing requires reflection, time to think through our thoughts and reward slow thinkers like me. I wish more people would think before they talk, and wait until they have something to add to a conversation. The world might then be a whole lot quieter for us thinkers.

Here's some writing advice my editor once shared, the best I've heard: A good newspaper column is like a letter written to a good friend—intimate, yet demanding; truth in an honest, revealing way. A good writer lives with a certain amount of risk, going beyond the surface into real emotions—things you'd share with a good friend.

In letters our private thoughts go public, a liberating feeling as writer reaches out to connect with reader. Not all letters need be sent. Some are meant to remain secrets. I can choose not to send a letter, which isn't an option in conversations. How often have we wanted to take back something we said? My thinking out loud has gotten me in trouble during a conversation, but unsent letters have helped me work through an emotion and recognize when something is better left unspoken.

Today, letters still count. Surrounded by high technology, the Internet, cell phones, text messaging and computers, we now use email as a major means of communication. Old-fashioned letter writing, words that matter. A simple truth remains: Good writing gets read and answered first.

This is how I'll write my letter to you. I'll start with something real, not abstract, a story that's anchored in the everyday and ordinary. No need to make up something. Life in our valley is filled with powerful memories, the ingredients a good cook starts with.

Then I'll explore with my senses. If I want to write about our family farm, I'll start with the earth and the rich aroma of turned soil or the taste of dust that filled our lungs. This is about a real farm and real work.

At some point I'll need to do some reading and research, looking over old notes, verifying details because I want to get things right. When I write about our family history, I want to make sure you know your great-grandfather arrived in 1899 from Japan and worked in the fields, unable to legally buy farmland because he was classified an "Oriental."

Often before I write, I warm up with great writers, reading their words and slipping into their rhythms. I listen to their voices and find comfort, like a good cup of coffee before the workday begins.

Gradually I'll start a list of words, key words that capture thoughts and feelings, good ones that can develop into phrases and sentences and eventually ideas with a life of their own. Some of these words I'll set aside; they may require more thought or they may not fit.

Finally, I hope my letter will convey my belief that anything in life worth doing must be done with passion. So I'll work with words carefully, my stories written with conviction. If I want you to remember my stories and commit them to memory, I can't afford to be vague and indifferent. I must honor a commitment to words, words I care about, of which I claim ownership.

Living in the Central Valley can make you invisible. We're the "other California" in a state and nation dominated by sound bites, where responses are often based on speed and anchored in quick wit. Our voices are easily lost. As a result, we too often let others speak for us and are perceived to have little to say.

Letters provide us with a voice, a slower, thoughtful voice in contrast with big-city rhythms. I'd like to think content still matters, that it's OK to go a little slower and think before we speak; talk more, shout less. Perhaps letters help us from feeling so inferior. They have helped me find my voice in a world dominated by aggressive talk.

So, my children, look for a letter sometime in the future. In the end, I believe life is all about loving. And loving words.

Your dad

AUTHOR ACKNOWLEDGMENTS

While writing may be a solitary act, the act of creating often includes others—especially, in my case, my family. My parents still provide me with inspiration and the absolute belief in my work only parents can offer. Thanks to my wife, Marcy, who kindly listens to my stories and usually nods her head in support, even when the writing is bad. And to my children, Nikiko and Korio, who have become part of this book and the letters I have written, letters I leave behind.

Special thanks to all the folks at Heyday Books—in particular Patricia Wakida and Jeannine Gendar with the help of Sarah Neidhardt. Heyday is a very special place—an oasis, an island—in the sea of books and publishing, a place where writing can be fun. Malcolm Margolin, publisher at Heyday, has become the friend all writers hope for, with stimulating conversations and a love of books, words and stories.

Elizabeth Wales continues to help in ways only a good friend and agent can.

I am grateful to the *Fresno Bee* and publisher Ray Steele, executive editor Charlie Waters and opinion editor Jim Boren for allowing my monthly columns in the *Bee* to be reprinted and shared in book form. No writer could have a better working relationship with a newspaper. Their vision has allowed my stories to gain new life.

Thanks to HarperCollins, publisher of *Epitaph for a Peach*, in which versions of "Lizard Dance" and "Spring Weeds" were originally published.

Also thanks to W. W. Norton and Company, publisher of my two other books, *Harvest Son* and *Four Seasons in Five Senses*, in which a version of "Scent of My Father" was originally published.

Working with Doug Hansen has been a treat—rarely does a writer get to work with the illustrator in such a fashion. We talk of art, stories and creativity, and his work advances each letter to another level. The craft of his art has made this book into a treasure.

Thanks to the many who have added to my letters—conversations and interviews, lending artifacts and objects for ideas and inspiration (from Kerry's baseball mitt to Hiro's uniform). For the moral support of many—I am grateful.

And to the people of the Central Valley and the readers of the *Fresno Bee* who offer support: Thank you for believing that words still carry meaning and reading still has a place in our world.

David Mas Masumoto
Author

My illustrations were first paired with the letters of Mas Masumoto in the Vision section of the *Fresno Bee*. I thank everyone who makes that continuing collaboration possible and successful: Ray Steele, Publisher; Charlie Waters, Executive Editor; Jim Boren, Opinion Editor, Gail Marshall, Associate Editor; Andrea Cooper, Art Director; and artists S. W. Parra and Gabriel Utasi.

At Heyday Books, Malcom Margolin, Publisher; Patricia Wakida, Special Project Development; and Rebecca LeGates, Art Director, evolved an elegant vision of what this book could be, and encouraged my participation in the process.

Most of the objects illustrated in the book were found on the Masumoto family farm. Dr. David Chesemore, professor of biology at California State University, Fresno, provided the western fence lizard illustrated in "Lizard Dance," and Kerry Nakagawa, director of the Nisei Baseball Research Project, generously loaned the authentic baseball glove that served as a model in "Baseball Saved Us."

I appreciate the warmth and generous spirit of Marcy, Nikiko and Korio Masumoto, who welcome me to their home without hesitation or reserve.

Finally, I acknowledge my good fortune to be associated with Mas Masumoto. It is a privilege to be treated as a partner by such an amiable and enterprising man, and an honor to share in the creation of this book of letters.

Doug Hansen
Illustrator

GREAT VALLEY BOOKS

Great Valley Books is a program of Heyday Institute, Berkeley. Books in the Great Valley series strive to publish, promote, and develop a deep appreciation of various aspects of the region's unique history and culture. Created in 2002 with a grant from The James Irvine Foundation, it strives to promote the rich literary, artistic, and cultural resources of California's Central Valley by publishing books of the highest merit and broadest interest.

A few of our Great Valley Books and other Central Valley titles include:

*Blithe Tomato*, by Mike Madison; *Haslam's Valley*, by Gerald Haslam; *Highway 99: A Literary Journey through California's Great Central Valley*, edited by Stan Yogi; and *Letters to the Valley: A Harvest of Memories*, by David Mas Masumoto.

For a complete list of Great Valley Books titles and information, please visit our website at www.heydaybooks.com/public/greatvalley.html.

GREAT
VALLEY

HEYDAY INSTITUTE

Since its founding in 1974, Heyday Books has occupied a unique niche in the publishing world, specializing in books that foster an understanding of California history, literature, art, environment, social issues, and culture. We are a 501(c)(3) nonprofit organization committed to providing a platform for writers, poets, artists, scholars, and storytellers who help keep California's diverse legacy alive.

We are grateful for the generous funding we've received for our publications and programs during the past year from various foundations and more than three hundred individuals. Major recent supporters include:

Anonymous; Anthony Andreas, Jr.; Arroyo Fund; Barnes & Noble bookstores; Bay Tree Fund; California Association of Resource Conservation Districts; California Oak Foundation; Candelaria Fund; Columbia Foundation; Colusa Indian Community Council; Wallace Alexander Gerbode Foundation; Richard & Rhoda Goldman Fund; Evelyn & Walter Haas, Jr. Fund; Walter & Elise Haas Fund; Hopland Band of Pomo Indians; James Irvine Foundation; Guy Lampard & Suzanne Badenhoop; Jeff Lustig; George Frederick Jewett Foundation; LEF Foundation; David Mas Masumoto; James McClatchy; Michael McCone; Gordon & Betty Moore Foundation; Morongo Band of Mission Indians; National Endowment for the Arts; National Park Service; Ed Penhoet; Poets & Writers; Rim of the World Interpretive Association; River Rock Casino; Alan Rosenus; San Francisco Foundation; John-Austin Saviano/ Moore Foundation; Sandy Cold Shapero; Ernest & June Siva; L.J. Skaggs and Mary C. Skaggs Foundation; Swinerton Family Fund; Susan Swig Watkins; and the Harold & Alma White Memorial Fund.

For more information about Heyday Institute, our publications and programs, please visit our website at www.heydaybooks.com.